T0210268

SCHIRMER'S LIBRARY
OF MUSICAL CLASSICS

Vol. 245

J. CONCONE

The School of Sight-Singing

Practical Method for Young Beginners

Followed by a Series of Favorite Melodies
Serving as Solfeggi

Arranged and Edited by
B. LÜTGEN

ISBN 978-0-7935-5102-6

G. SCHIRMER, *Inc.*

Printed in the U.S.A. by G. Schirmer, Inc.

First Series of Solfeggi.

Before singing the following Exercises in time, it is necessary to study each note of the scale separately, in order to acquire a good emission of the voice, faultless intonation, and purity and unbroken continuity of vocal tone.

Duple* (or Common) time marked by a **C**.

In quicker movements($^{2}/_{2}$ time, with 2 beats to the measure) this sign is crossed: **₵**.

The commas(,) are breathing-marks.

Scale in Whole notes.

One whole note in the measure.

*) There are two classes of Time, *Duple* and *Triple*. In *Duple* time, the number of beats to the measure is divisible by 2; in *Triple* time, by 3.

Printed in the U.S.A. by G. Schirmer, Inc.

Take breath during each rest and at the sign (,).

Exercise on Major and Minor seconds.

4.

Make the pupil sing the following three notes: [music: 1. 2. 3.] After this, strike the third: [music: 1, 3,], and let him become acquainted with that Interval.

Make the pupil sing
1, 2, 3, 4.
and become acquainted with the Interval of the Fourth:
1, 4.
Exercise on fourths.
6.
Fifth.
1, 2, 3, 4, 5.
Fifth.
1, 5.
Exercise on fifths.
7.

Sixth.
1, 2, 3, 4, 5, 6.
1, 6.
Exercise on Sixths.
8.

The Major Seventh (composed of 5 tones and one semitone) ascends, and leads to the Octave; the Minor Seventh (4 tones and 2 semitones) descends.

Major 7th ascends.
1, 2, 3, 4, 5, 6, 7.
1, 7, 8.

Minor 7th descends.
1, 2, 3, 4, 5, 6, 7.
1, 7, 6.

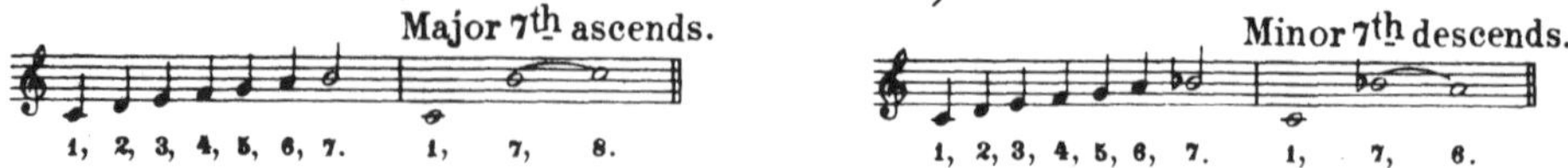

Exercise on Octaves and Major and Minor Sevenths.

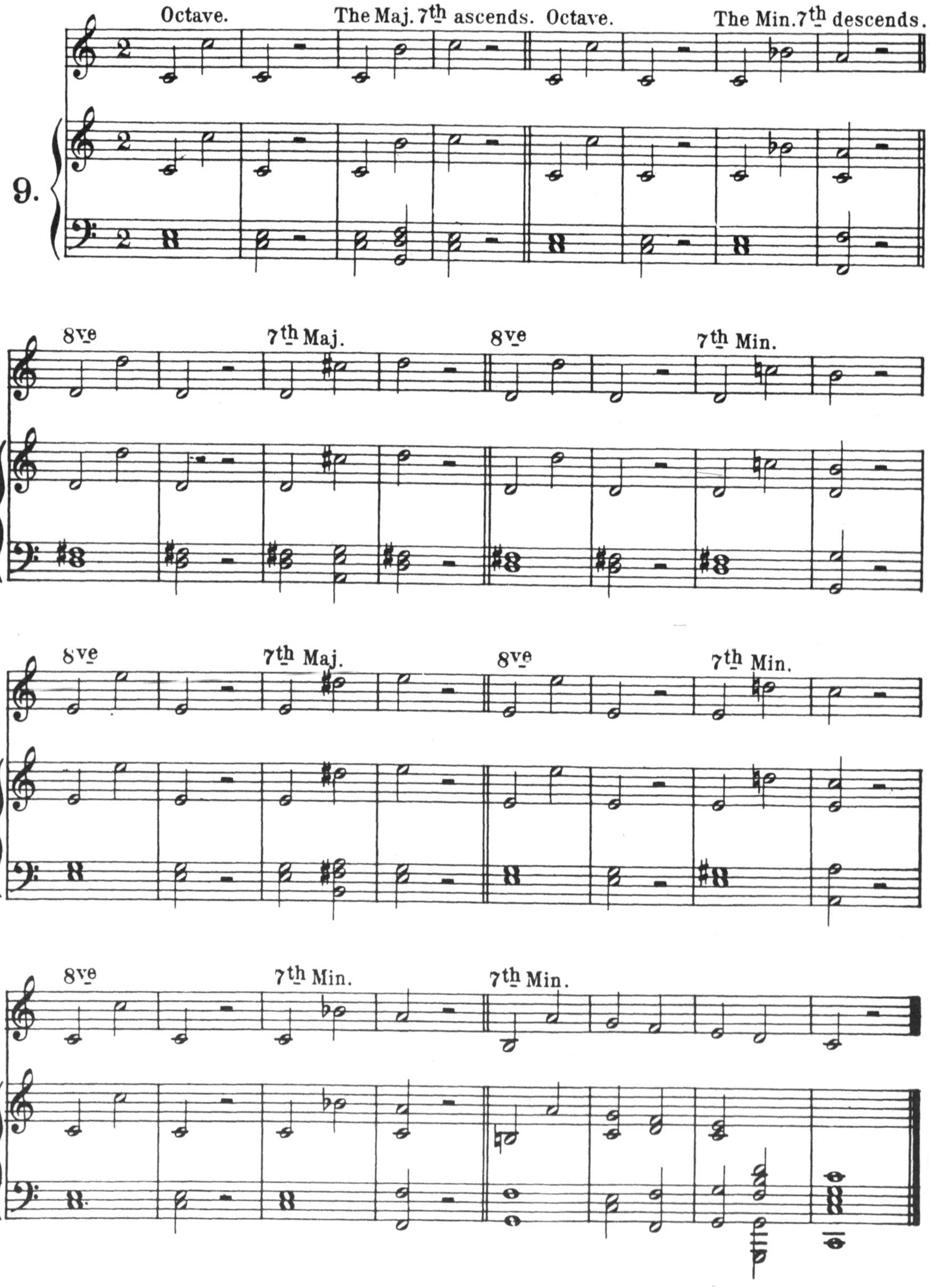
Octave.
The Maj. 7th ascends.
Octave.
The Min. 7th descends.
9.
8ve
7th Maj.
8ve
7th Min.
8ve
7th Maj.
8ve
7th Min.
8ve
7th Min.
7th Min.

Before the pupil attempts the singing of any lesson, he must be sure of the names of the notes, so that his attention be not withdrawn from the proper intonation of the Intervals and the right division of time.

Note. In the Musical Academies and public Singing-Classes in France, where *reading at sight* forms the basis of all musical education, a highly commendable preliminary exercise is employed, called "la lecture rhythmique" (rhythmical reading); it consists in naming the notes aloud, and strictly in time, which is marked by even movements of the hand.

*) This curved line (‿ or ⁀) is called a Tie. When two or more notes on the same line or in the same space are connected by a tie, the second note must not be repeated, the sound of the first one being prolonged for the time-value of all the notes so tied.

The sharps are generally placed in the following order

Some composers put the first sharp between the 1st and 2nd line, which makes the succession of sharps appear more regular to the eye ; but the former mode is preferable.

Moderato.

1 2 1 2

12.

Moderato.

1 2 1 2

13.

Moderato.
1 2 3 4
14.

Andante.
1 2 3 4
15.

Triple Time.

Three quarter-notes in a measure (or any combination of notes forming together $3/4$ of a whole note).

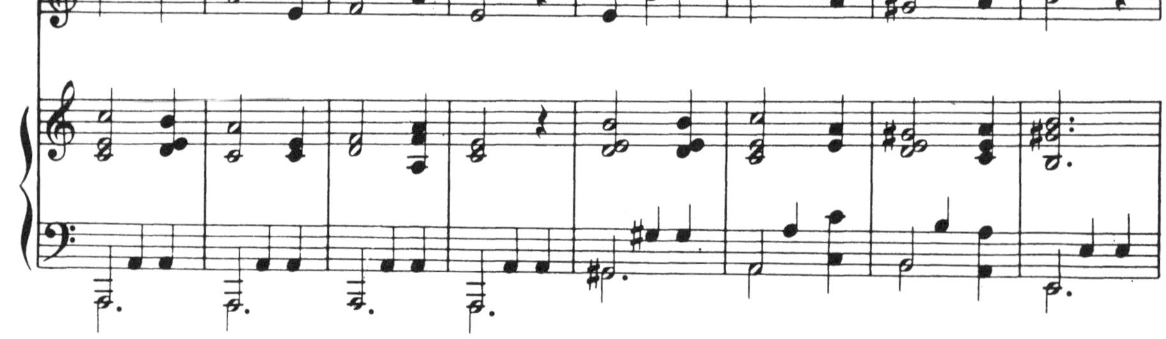

Lento.
17.
1 2 3 1 2 3

Two-four Time. (2/4)

Two quarter-notes (or their corresponding value) in a measure.

Andantino.
19.
1 2 1 2

Triple Time. (3/8)

Three eighth-notes (or their corresponding value) in a measure.

Andantino.

1 2 3 1 2 3

20

Second Series of Lessons.

In the first Series the accompaniment helps the pupil; in the second Series he is expected to be certain of his intonation. It is advisable to let him try each lesson without accompaniment.

Dotted Half-notes.

The dot after a note increases its time-value by one-half.

A dotted half-note is thus equal to a half-note plus a quarter-note, or to three quarter-notes.

Dotted Quarter-notes.

A dotted quarter-note is equal in time-value to three eighth-notes.

Andantino.
24.
1 2 1 2 1 2 1 2

Andante.
1 2 3
1 2 3
25.

Syncopation.

The pupil has already been told that, when two notes on the same degree are united by a Tie ⌒, the second must not be repeated; the first note is simply prolonged by the time-value of the second. When a note is thus *tied over* a strong beat in a measure from a weak beat in the same (or a preceding) measure, the rhythmic effect produced is termed *syncopation*.

EXAMPLES.

Example I.

Ex. II. Usual notation.

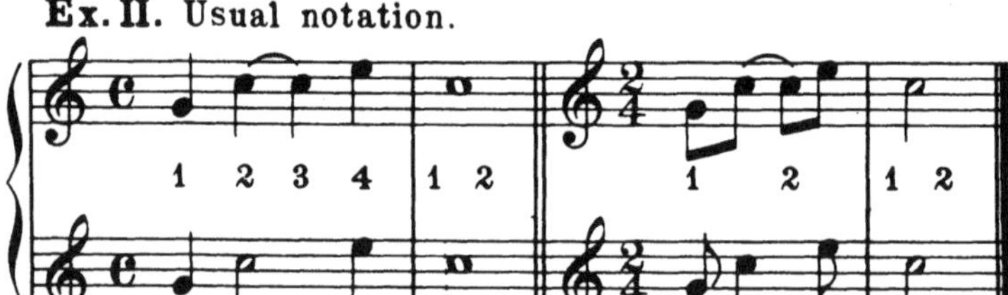

Ex. III. Succession of syncopated notes.

The same with notes of different value.

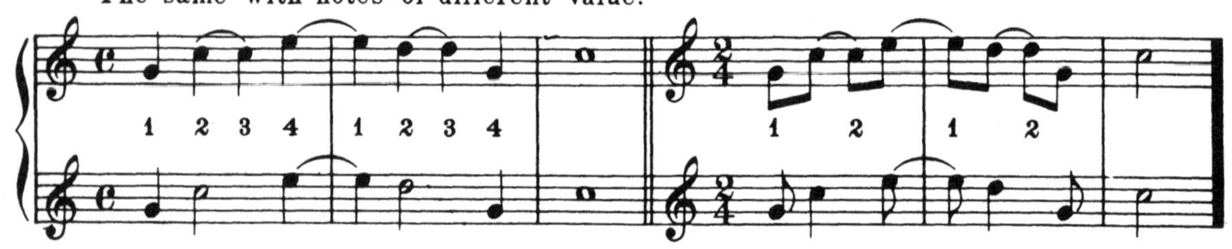

Ex. IV. Syncopation in Triple Time.

Ex. V.

The following numerous Exercises on Syncopation, (in which the syncopated notes must be attacked without hesitation,) will enable the presevering pupil to overcome one of the greatest difficulties in music.

Do not pass from one Exercise to the following one, until you can execute it without hesitation.

Andante. In Triple Time.
1 2 3 1 2 3
32.
Andantino.
33.

Allegretto.
34.
Fine.
Subito. D. C.

Allegretto.
1 2 3
1 2 3
35.
poco rallent. - - a tempo.
poco rallent. - - a tempo.
rallent.
rallent.

Andante.
1 2 3 4
1 2 3 4
1 2 3 4
36.

Expression-marks.

The modifications of tone required in the performance of musical compositions are indicated by the following Italian words (or their abbreviations).

Piano (by abbreviation ***p***) signifies: softly.

Pianissimo (by abbreviation ***pp***) signifies: very softly.

Crescendo (*cresc.*, or <): swelling, increasing in loudness.

Decrescendo, or diminuendo (*dim.*, or >): decreasing in loudness.

Forte (***f***): strong, loud.

Fortissimo (***ff***): very loud.

Smorzando (*smorz.*): softening gradually.

Morendo: expiring.

Sostenuto (*sost.*): sustained.

Legato, Legatissimo: smooth, very smooth.

Staccato, Staccatissimo: detached, very detached.

The smooth or connected style, *Legato,* is also marked by a Slur for several notes or whole measures.

Staccato is marked by dots placed over the notes.

Sometimes the rapidity of the movement must be modified; the different indications are:

Rallentando (*rall.*) }: Retarding the movement.
Ritardando (*rit.* or *ritard.*) }

Accelerando (*accel.*) }: Hastening the movement.
Stringendo (*string.*) }

Third Series.

Compound Time.

Besides the two main classes of time, there are two subclasses, *Compound Duple time* and *Compound Triple time.* In *compound duple time* the number of beats to each measure is still divisible by 2, but *each beat* contains, instead of an ordinary note divisible by 2, a *dotted* note (or its equivalent in other notes or rests) divisible by 3; hence the term *compound,* each simple beat being represented by a *dotted* or *compound* note divisible by 3, instead of a simple note divisible by 2. In *compound triple time* not only the number of beats in each measure is divisible by 3, but also *each beat.*

By dividing the numerator by 3, the pupil will find immediately how the Time must be counted.

Thus 6/4, 6/8, or 6/16 time (compound duple times) is counted *one, two,* because 6 contains twice 3.

12/4, 12/8, or 12/16 time (also compound duple times) is counted *one, two, three, four.*

9/4, 9/8, or 9/16 time (compound triple times) is counted *one, two, three.*

Theme with Variations.

Review of the preceding Exercises.

Theme with Variations.

Review of the preceding Exercises.

Common Time.
Allegro giusto.
1 2 3 4
41.

Compound Duple Time.

(Here four dotted quarter-notes are equal to twelve eighth-notes.)

Andantino.
43.
1 2 1 2
Fine.
poco.
poco.
D. C.
D. C.

Two dotted quarter-notes are equal to six eighth-notes.

Andante espressivo.

1 2 1 2 1 2

44.

Simple Triple Time.

Three quarter-notes in a measure.

Compound Triple Time.
Three dotted quarter-notes are equal to nine eighth-notes.
Lento.
1 2 3
46.

Special Exercise on Augmented Seconds and Minor Thirds.

This Lesson shows the difference between *Legato* and *Staccato*.

Triplets.

Triplets and Double Triplets.

When Double Triplets are marked by a 6, they are divided into three times two, instead of twice three.

dim. pp dim. pp

cresc. dim. rall. cresc. dim. rall.

52. Andante religioso.

HAYDN. 1732-1809.

dolce. p p

cresc.

cresc. p dim. rf rf

Andante.
LULLI. 1633-1687.
53.
dolce.
cresc.
dolce.
mf
riten.
Andante espressivo.
B. KLEIN. 1794-1832.
54.
p
sf
mf
cresc.
dim. e rall.

Allegretto giocoso.
WEBER.
55.
mf
p
f
rfz
mf
cresc.
f
f
f
Andantino.
WINTER. 1754-1825.
56.
poco cresc.
poco cresc.
mf
mf
p
sfz

Allegro.
Popular German song.
57.
p leggiero.
cresc.
rfz
Resignation.
Andante con moto.
58.
cresc.
rit.
a tempo.
p dolce.

più *f*

più *f*

p

cresc.

f

rit.

a tempo.

espress.

cresc.

f

rit.

p

f

p

cresc.

pp

Lento. FR. SCHUBERT. 1797-1828.

59.

dolce.

pp

pp

Andante poco Adagio.
DALAYRAC. 1753-1809.
60.
p espressivo.
p
riten.
a tempo.
cresc.
mf
mf
a tempo.
p
riten.
Tempo I.
dolce.
cresc.
ad lib.

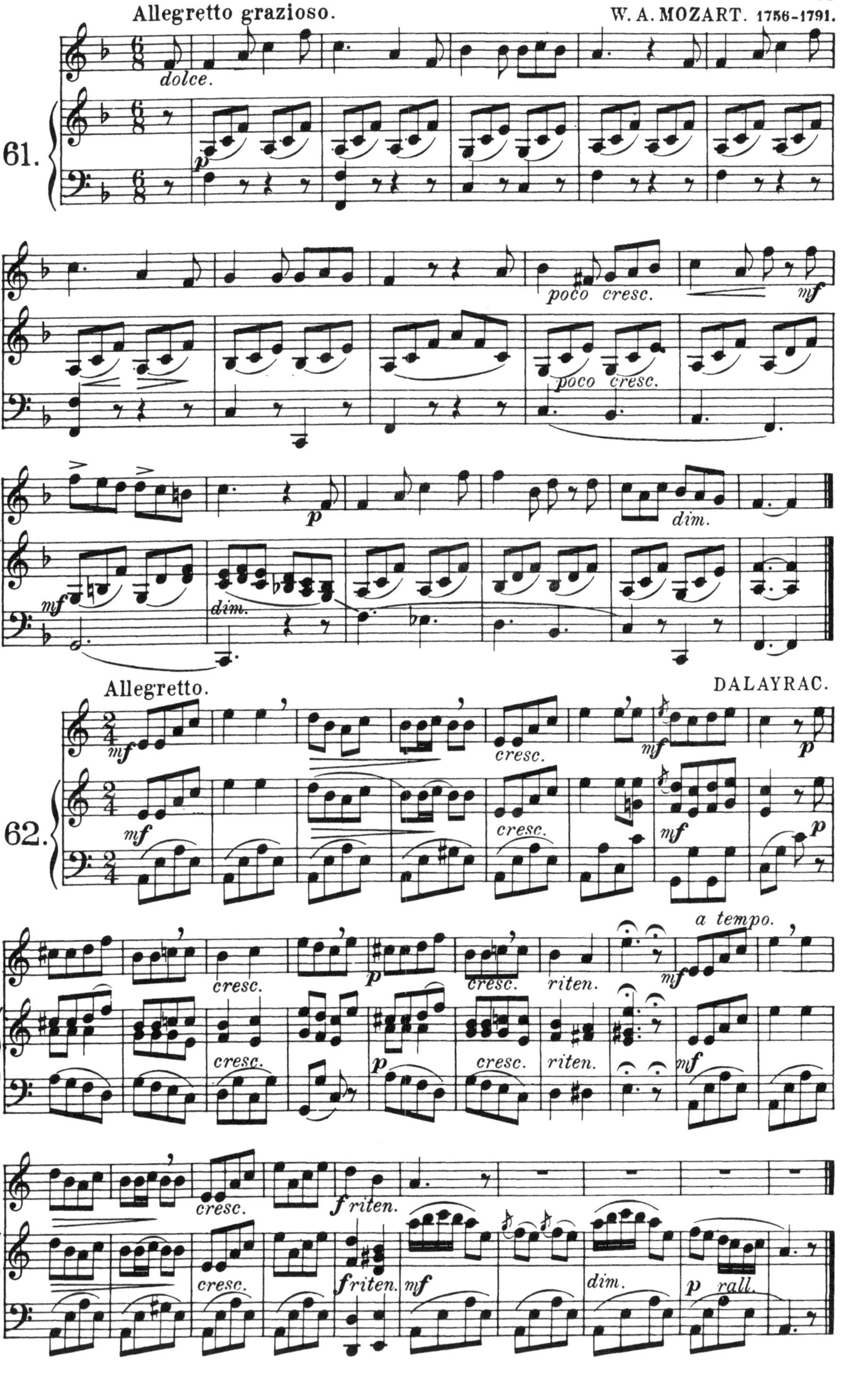
Allegretto grazioso.
W. A. MOZART. 1756-1791.
61.
dolce.
p
poco cresc.
poco cresc.
mf
mf
dim.
p
dim.
Allegretto.
DALAYRAC.
62.
mf
cresc.
p
cresc.
riten.
a tempo.
f riten.
mf
dim.
p rall.

Allegretto grazioso.
NAEGELI.
à due.
dolce.
63.
p dolce.
Solo.
Fine.
Fine.
mf
poco cresc.
mf
dim.
D. C.
poco cresc.
mf
D. C.
Andantino.
MOZART.
dolce.
64.
p

cresc.
cresc.
rall.
Andantino espressivo.
H. WERNER.
65.
pp
pp
mf poco cresc.
f
dolce.
dim.

Poco Adagio
DALAYRAC.
66.
dolce.
dolce.
riten.
riten.
f
mf
mf
riten.
riten.
dolce.
dolce.
cresc.
cresc.
mf
mf
dolce.
dolce.
cresc.
cresc.
riten.
riten..

Larghetto.
67.
Canzonetta napoletana.
Andantino.
68.

mf
p
mf
Larghetto
From "Preciosa."
WEBER.
dolce.
legato.
69.
p
dolce
riten.
Andante con moto.
WEBER.
dolce.
70.
dolce.

riten.
riten.

La Carolina.

Canzonetta napoletana.

Allegretto.

71.

La Romanesca.

Fameux Air de Danse de la fin du XVIème Siècle.

Moderato,

più lento.
riten.
più lento.
riten.

From "Oberon."

Allegro. WEBER.

f
p
p
cresc.
mf
cresc.
mf
f
p
riten.
riten.
ff